# The
# Happy Mom
# Mindset

## WORKBOOK

# MOLLY CLAIRE

ISBN-13:
978-1548508449

ISBN-10:
1548508446

For bulk purchase and for booking, contact:

molly@mollyclaire.com
www.mollyclaire.com

# CONTENTS

GETTING STARTED                         1

MOM AUTOPILOT                           7

ALWAYS ON CALL                         19

MOM COMPARISON                         35

MAKE THEM HAPPY                        45

MAKING THEM SUCCEED                    57

A VICTIM OF MOTHERHOOD                 67

WHAT ABOUT MOM?                        75

ABOUT THE AUTHOR                       99

# GETTING STARTED

## Consistency

Is consistency a challenge? Let's uncover your thoughts about it.

- On a scale of 1 to 10, how difficult is consistency for you?

- What gets in the way of you being consistent when you commit to something?

- Think of a time in the past when you were able to be consistent with a goal. Write about it:

- Why do you believe you were able to be consistent?

- What can you learn from that experience?

- How might you use that experience of success as evidence that you can be consistent today or in the future?

## The Unexpected

Motherhood = The Unexpected. How does the unexpected impact you? Let's find out.

- How challenging is it for you when things don't go as planned?

- Tell me about an example of when it's been easy for you to adapt:

- Tell me about an example of when it's been challenging for you to adapt:

- What do you perceive as the difference between the two?

- If you could embrace the unexpected more often, how might your life change?

- What needs to change in your mindset in order to achieve that?

## Where Are You?

When it comes to your own life, where are you, and where do you want to be? Let's check in.

- What are the three best things about your life right now?

- Why do you believe you have those things in your life?

- What is missing from your life now?

- Why is that so challenging for you?

## Where Are You? (continued)

- What changes would you like to make?

- Do you believe those changes are possible?

- What's one thing you want to change as a result of reading *The Happy Mom Mindset*?

# MOM AUTOPILOT

## Is It Hard to Say No?

- On a scale from 1 to 10, how hard is it for you to say "no" to something asked of you?

- How do you determine what is a "no" and what is a "yes" in your life?

- Saying "no" means I'm _____.

- Saying "yes" means I'm _____.

- Would it benefit you if you were able to say "no" more easily? Why or why not?

- How would your life be different if saying "no" was an option more often?

## Less on the List—Let's Visualize

This is a time for you to visualize. Understanding what's possible helps us make drastic changes.

- How would your life change if you had less on your "list" every day?

- How would you feel if you had a lighter schedule?

- How would your relationships be different?

- What else would be possible for your life?

- With less on your list, what would you be most proud of?

## Less on the List—Feeling Resistant?

Let's face it: Cutting the list down can be a challenge. Let's find out why, where, and how you're stuck.

- The hardest thing about clearing my list is:

- If this weren't a problem, then I would:

- One idea I have to overcome this obstacle is:

- What I most fear about clearing my list is:

- It would be much easier to eliminate "to dos" if:

- It would be worth it to make these changes if I knew that:

## Priorities

Today you are creating five "big picture" priorities using these questions as a guide. These are the basic five priorities, but you can use these same questions to create five sub-priorities under any one of these "big picture" priorities.

Remember, just because something is a higher priority doesn't mean it will take more of your time than anything else. It just means that it will be given *enough* time.

Make a list of your top five priorities in order.

1.

2.

3.

4.

5.

## Priorities (continued)

- Why did you put them in this order? Why is your #1 priority so important to you?

- How do you feel about your list?

- Are you currently living in line with these priorities? Think about what you did yesterday; does it reflect the order of these priorities?

## Questioning Your List: The Guide

Your list does not need to run your life. You're in charge. You get to decide.

Take your list for the day with all of your home, family, and personal needs, and get ready to ask some questions. (You can ask similar questions for your list at work too).

Look at the list and ask:

- What do I NEED to do on this list?

- Why do I need to do them?

- What do I WANT to do on this list? Why do I want to do them?

- What on this list can/should someone else do?

- Does this list align with my priorities?

## Questioning Your List: The Guide  (continued)

- If not, what can fall off the list?

Use these questions with your list every day. Keep these questions in your mind as well.

When your kids expect or ask something of you, question in your mind if it is REALLY something you need to do. Let the criteria above be the judge. Write these questions down where you will see them regularly. Practice them. Then practice them again.

**Feelings**

This is an area for you to record any feelings you notice with this process. Guilt? Freedom? Hesitation? Excitement? Fear? Write them down. You'll learn so much about yourself!

## Curiosity: The Solve-Every-Problem Solution

• When your kids start to unload or tell you about a problem, how do you feel?

• What thoughts do you have that create these feelings?

• When your kids start to unload or tell you about a problem, what do you do?

• Do you think this is productive? Why or why not?

• Is listening more and problem solving less something you would find beneficial? Why or why not?

**Extra Help**

If you fall into solving every problem, here are a few questions to keep handy. Use these questions as a guide, and constantly remind yourself of them when your child comes to you with a problem or frustration. What other questions can you add to this list that you might find helpful?

1.  Does my child need my help? Or do they want me to listen?

2.  Did I ask if they need or want my help?

3.  Is this an opportunity to let them problem solve?

4.  What is my responsibility here?

## Your CTFAR Models

Let's take a look at some of your thought models. When you write down the circumstance, make sure it reflects only the facts about your situation with no added opinion. The result will always be your result, not anyone else's.

- Circumstance:

- Thought:

- Feeling:

- Action:

- Result:

# ALWAYS ON CALL

## Questions for "Dr. Mom"

If you relate to the description of Dr. Mom, I've got some questions just for you! This is a way to get you thinking about what your current patterns are creating and if you like those results.

- Does it benefit your kids that you are always available? Why or why not?

- Is always being "on call" what you want to do? Why or why not?

- Do you see any benefit to creating your own schedule first? Why or why not?

- What (if any) advantages might there be if your kids knew they needed to ask you for something in advance?

## Questions for "Dr. Mom" (continued)

- What (if any) advantages might there be if there were times that your kids needed to find another solution because you aren't available?

- What (if any) advantages might there be if your kids understood that you had needs and a schedule as well?

## Questions for "Annoyed Mom"

If you relate to the description of Annoyed Mom, I've got some questions just for you! This is a way to get you thinking about what your current patterns are creating and if you like those results.

- Have you really given yourself permission to have your own schedule? Tell me about it:

- On a scale from 1 to 10, how much guilt do you feel when you have your own plans?

- Is setting limits on your time a challenge for you?

- Are you allowed to have your own schedule? Why or why not?

- Are there benefits to your kids working around your schedule? Why or why not?

## Questions for "Frazzled Mom"

If you relate to the description of Frazzled Mom, I've got some questions just for you! This is a way to get you thinking about what your current patterns are creating and if you like those results.

- When do you allow urgency to take your attention away from what's important?

- Why do you allow urgency to take your attention away from what's important?

- What would it be like if the things that were important always kept your attention?

- How would your life change?

- Who would benefit from it and how?

## Intentional Life Brainstorm

When your life is intentional, you are creating what you want in life. You are creating the relationship you want with your kids and everyone else. You are creating the environment and opportunities you want. You are showing your kids what it's like to make a decision about what you want in life and make it happen. Modeling your own intentional life and the resulting success is one of the *best* ways to teach your child to create their own success.

- Think about what an Intentional Life means to you. Describe what YOUR intentional life looks like:

- What are the thoughts and feelings driving your current time management (or lack thereof)?

- Describe what your life would be like if you were better at being intentional with your time:

- Would better time management affect the way you feel each day? Why or why not?

- Would it affect your family? How?

## Intentional Life Brainstorm (continued)

- Would it impact your other responsibilities?

- Would better time management make a positive difference in your life? Why or why not?

## Protecting Your Time

Protecting your time is one of the BEST things you can do. Why? When you are able to protect your time, your space, and your emotional well-being, you will be more relaxed, more energetic, happier, and more INTENTIONAL. Isn't that the kind of woman you want to be?

Protecting your time also helps your kids. It teaches them to plan ahead. It teaches them to take initiative and responsibility. It teaches them to respect your time as well as the time of others.

- Do you believe you have permission to protect your time? Why or why not?

- Where in your life would you most benefit from protecting your time? Why?

- What limits can you put in place to protect it?

- What fears do you have around setting these limits?

## Protecting Your Time (continued)

- What feelings might get in the way of your setting and sticking to these limits?

- What are the thoughts or beliefs causing these feelings?

## Urgent vs. Important

How often do you allow things that are "urgent" to dictate your time instead of what's *important*? Use your list of priorities to help you determine what's urgent vs. important. These questions will help you get a glimpse into your current patterns and what they are creating.

- List here "urgent" things that regularly pull your attention away from important things:

- Why do you allow urgency to take your attention?

- In what ways is this affecting your life?

- Describe in detail what it would be like if things that were IMPORTANT always kept your attention. How would your life change?

## Urgent vs. Important (continued)

- Is making a change to stay focused on what's important something you want to commit to? Why or why not?

- If you pursue this change, what obstacles do you foresee getting in the way?

- Are you willing to move past these obstacles? Why or why not?

- If so, how will you overcome them?

## Time Journal Prompt

For the next 24 to 48 hours, please keep a time journal. This is a great way to notice how you are spending your time. You'll also discover when and how you lose track of time, when you are most productive, and where you need to focus as you create a time system.

Use this sheet to keep notes and reflect on your discoveries. Understanding what's happening now is important information as you make decisions about what you want to change. When you are finished, you can use the reflection questions.

## Time Journal: Let's Reflect

Now that you've documented how you use your time, use these questions to reflect:

- When are you most productive?

- What gets in the way of your being productive? What thoughts or feelings come up?

- Is your time aligning with your priorities? Why or why not?

- What adjustments can you make to help time better align with your priorities?

## Time Journal Prompt (continued)

- What surprised you the most about your time journal?

- Additional thoughts or observations:

## Do the Math

Getting mathematical about your time is powerful. Instead of focusing on "so much to do" or something that will "take forever," find out exactly what you have to do and how long it will take. Get specific and use a calendar to record what you need to do. Put an end to the drama around time.

- List here everything on your list in detail. If you're doing a big project, break down each step. Be specific.

- Go back to the list above and write down exactly how much time you anticipate each step taking.

- Get out your calendar and schedule each item like an appointment.

- Create a time frame for overflow to accommodate for the unexpected. Be specific with your time, but allow for error and unknowns that will come up.

- What do you notice about how you feel with each item quantified and scheduled?

## Resistance to Time Management

If you resist managing your time, let's find out why.

* Time management is _____.

* The reason I don't manage my time is because _____.

* Managing my time would be much easier if _____.

* If I believed I could manage my time, then I would feel _____.

* The thing that would really motivate me to do a better job of time management is_____.

* Is making an effort for better time management worth it to you? Why or why not?

## Thoughts about Time

What do you think about time? Not enough? Too short? Hard to manage? Let's find out what's happening in that brain. The way you think about time will create your experience of time.

- List three things you regularly say or think about time:

- For each one, describe how they make you feel:

- How would you like to feel about the time you have each day?

- What would you need to believe in order to feel that way about it?

- If you did think and feel that way about time, what do you imagine would happen?

# MOM COMPARISON

## "The List"

This space is provided for you to write "the list." This is a comprehensive list of all the things you expect of yourself as a "good" mom. Think about how you would finish the sentence, "A good mom will . . ." and write down everything that applies. Keep going until you can think of nothing else!

## The Right Mom

It's common for women to feel inadequate as moms, and it's usually because they doubt their own abilities. Believing that you are called and qualified to be exactly the mom your kids need is really powerful. Let's see what your thoughts are about who the "right mom" is for your kids.

- In what ways do you think you are the perfect mom for your kids?

- How does it feel when you think about these things?

- When, where, and how do feelings of inadequacy come up for you?

- What are the thoughts that cause you to feel inadequate?

## The Right Mom (continued)

- What would be different if you knew today without a doubt that you are the exact mom your kids need?

- Do you want to believe that? Why or why not?

## Do It All

It's easy to fall into the trap of believing we should do it all. We may even think we want to do it all! What we really want are the feelings we believe we will experience when we are doing it all. We believe that we'll feel good about ourselves, at peace with how we are doing, and assured that our kids will turn out okay. You can create these feelings for yourself, and it never requires you to "do it all." Doing it all usually gets in the way of the optimal experience.

• What do you think about the idea of "doing it all" ?

• How often do you feel inadequate or guilty because you're not doing it all?

• What other emotions do you experience?

• If you could do it all, would you want to? Why or why not?

## Do It All (continued)

- How do you imagine you'd feel if you could "do it all" ?

- How would your life improve if you could live from those feelings now?

## Fear of Missing Out

Fear of missing out convinces us to overspend, overextend, and create unnecessary stress. Let's take a look at where you are experiencing this phenomenon so you can clear it out.

- In what area do you fear that you or your kids are missing out?

- Is it true that you're missing out? Give some details:

- Is it helpful for you to fear that you're missing out? Why or why not?

- In what ways are you or your kids gaining something in this experience rather than missing out?

- If you didn't believe you or your kids were missing out, would you still want to do this particular activity? Why or why not?

## Making Decisions You Feel Good About

Learning how to make decisions you feel good about regardless of other people's opinions is so freeing. In order to know what you want to do, it's essential to understand what's important to you.

- Think about how you spend your time on a daily basis. Write things down that matter to you personally:

- Now write down things that matter to other people:

- Go ahead and write down the things you think you "should" do that you just haven't questioned.

- When you look at these lists, what things might you consider removing from your life?

## Making Decisions You Feel Good About (continued)

- What fears do you have around doing so?

- How might you overcome those?

## Questions

Powerful questions are a great way to help your brain make a U turn away from a negative thought spiral. Questions like, "What's perfect about this?" "What's the good news?" or "How can I create what I want?" are a few of my favorites. Go ahead and answer these questions to come up with your own.

- How do you want to feel on a regular basis in your life?

- What kinds of thoughts or beliefs create those feelings for you?

- Think of two questions that will lead your brain down the pathway to those thoughts and feelings. Write them here.

- If you use these questions regularly, what might happen for you?

- Where can you put these questions so you'll remember to use them on a regular basis?

# MAKE THEM HAPPY

## Your Child's Happiness

Your child's happiness is really up to them. Let's take some inventory and see how much you are feeling the responsibility of "fixing" their emotions.

- On a scale from 1 to 10, how difficult is it when your child is unhappy? Tell me more about this:

- How much influence do you believe you have over your child's happiness? Explain:

- If you *could* "make" your kids happy, would you want that job? Why or why not?

- How much do you think your kids expect you to make them happy? Tell me more about this:

- What is it like for you when you want your kids to be happy but they aren't?

## Your Child's Happiness (continued)

- When you think about allowing your kids to feel however they choose, what is that like for you?

- How would your life or relationships be different if everyone in your family was only responsible for their own emotional state?

## Taking Responsibility for Your Feelings

There is never a time when you are not responsible for how you feel. You might be faced with a circumstance or a person who you believe is causing your feelings, but you are always the one who is deciding how to feel. It is not what happens to you; it is what you believe about what happens to you that causes the feeling.

- Name a person or circumstance you believe is causing the negative feeling:

- Describe how they are making you feel:

- Describe why you think they have the power to create your feelings in this way:

- Describe your feeling without the influence of this person or circumstance (what you would be feeling if they hadn't "made" you feel this way):

- What is the thought you are thinking that is causing this feeling:

## Separating Out the Facts

When facing a situation that seems to be causing you to feel frustration or upset, it's really useful to separate out the facts. It will help you get clear on what's actually happening and what your perception of the situation is. So often we make facts mean something more than what they really do. Use these questions to help you separate out the facts.

- Describe a stressful or painful situation you are currently dealing with. Describe it in detail:

- Now list just the facts of the situation:

- Now list your opinions and thoughts about these facts:

- How is your added opinion or interpretation causing you to feel?

- Can you see how your interpretation of the facts is why you feel the way you do—not the facts themselves?

## Finding Useful Thoughts

Useful thoughts are those that create something good for you. A thought can be "positive" but still not create the result you want. A useful thought simply needs to be effective at creating the feelings you want to drive the right kind of action.

Here are a few questions to help you come up with some:

- Think of a situation that is a challenge for you and write about it here:

- What are your thoughts about it?

- What are some of the feelings these thoughts create?

- How would you like to feel in this situation?

## Finding Useful Thoughts (continued)

• What are some truths or beliefs that will create that feeling for you?

• How can you use those truths or beliefs in a useful way to help you problem solve?

## Bridging Thoughts

A bridging thought is a useful thought that is fairly neutral. It helps you bridge your current way of thinking to the way of thinking you want to adopt. For example, rather than forcing the thought, "I'm a good mom," you can use the thought, "I have a desire to be a good mom." This helps you move toward a better way of thinking gradually. Go ahead and create your own here.

• Write down a thought or thought pattern you want to change:

• What is this thought creating?

• How would you like to be able to think instead?

• What would that new line of thinking create for you?

• What is a thought that can bridge these two?

## Bridging Thoughts (continued)

- How does the new bridging thought feel to you?

- How will it help you make the changes you want?

## Questions for the CTFAR Model

This is a guide to help you find your CTFAR model. These questions will help you to fill it in and see what it's creating. Let's give it a try.

- How am I feeling?

- What am I thinking that's causing me to feel this way?

- When I feel _____, how does that make me want to react?

- If I take that action, what will likely happen?

## Questions for the CTFAR Model (continued)

Go ahead and fill in your CTFAR Model here:

- Circumstance (facts only):

- Thought:

- Feeling:

- Action:

- Result:

- Is this the model you want to have? Why or why not?

# MAKING THEM SUCCEED

## Allowing Your Kids to Own Their Results

- Think of a time when your child had great success. How did that feel to you?

- What were you thinking that created those feelings?

- Did you perceive this success to be a reflection on you or on your child? Tell me more about it:

- Think of a time when your child experienced failure or exhibited bad behavior. How did that feel to you?

- What were you thinking that created those feelings?

## Allowing Your Kids to Own Their Results (continued)

- Did you perceive this failure to be a reflection on you or your child? Tell me more about it:

- What would be different if you could separate your child's success from your own?

## Your Responsibility vs. Their Responsibility

Think of a scenario where you wish your child was having a different result. This could be academic, performance, behavior, or anything you consider to be an area in which they should "succeed."

• Why is it so frustrating that they are not achieving what you believe they should?

• In this scenario, what is your responsibility?

• In this scenario, what is your child's responsibility?

• What would it be like for you if you could only take responsibility for your part in this?

## Your Responsibility vs. Their Responsibility (continued)

• Can you think of any drawbacks of letting your child take responsibility for their part?

• Can you think of any benefits of letting your child take responsibility for their part?

## How Resilient Are You?

- Write something down that you perceive as a failure for you personally:

- When you think about this, what thoughts and feelings surface?

- Have you used this failure to your advantage in any way? Explain.

- What have you made this failure mean about you?

- Can you think of a time that failure has been beneficial in achieving a result?

## How Resilient Are You? (continued)

- Take a minute and imagine if each of your failures was like a personal package of the most valuable information you could receive. . . . What would that be like for you?

- If each failure was taking you one step closer to your success, would your perspective be different? How?

## Success and What Other People Think

Sometimes the hardest part about allowing our kids to fail and succeed on their own is what we believe other people will think. Let's check in on your perspective and how it's impacting you.

- Think of the last time your child "failed" or didn't meet a social standard. How did that feel to you?

- What were you thinking that caused you to feel that way?

- What did you fear others might be thinking?

- Why was it difficult for you to imagine them thinking that?

## Success and What Other People Think (continued)

- What would it be like if you could have experienced the same scenario without fear of judgement?

- How might your experience or the outcome have been different?

# A VICTIM OF
# MOTHERHOOD

## It's Not Fair

It's common for us to think that certain things in our life are "unfair." The problem with this line of thinking is that it keeps us feeling stuck and powerless. Let's take a look at where this is coming up for you and see what other options there might be.

- Think of a situation that seems unfair to you and write it here:

- When you think the thought, "it's unfair," how does that feel to you?

- Is it helpful to you to believe that this scenario is unfair? Why or why not?

- What if you weren't able to think that thought about the scenario at all? What might you think instead?

- What perspective might someone outside of the situation offer you?

## It's Not Fair (continued)

- If you could think differently about it, would you want to? Why or why not?

- What advice would you give someone else in this same situation?

## What They Deserve

When we get stuck believing that someone else deserves something negative, often we choose to feel and behave in a negative way to try to make that happen. It only creates more pain and negative results in our own lives. Here are a few questions to help you get unstuck:

- Think of someone you're upset with who you believe "deserves" for you to be angry:

- What is it exactly that you think they deserve?

- How do you feel when you think that they deserve that?

- Do you want to feel that way? Why or why not?

- Can you see that you are creating negative feelings for yourself in this situation?

## What They Deserve (continued)

- If you could feel more at peace with this situation, would you want to? Why or why not?

- What solutions can you see in this scenario that don't require you to experience these negative emotions?

## You Always Have a Choice

It's always refreshing to know that you have a choice. Even when the choice isn't optimal, owning a choice is always your best option for greater happiness. Let's practice owning some choices here.

- Think of a scenario in which you believe you don't have a choice and list it here:

- Is it true that you don't have a choice?

- What other options do you have than what you are currently choosing?

- What consequences go with each option?

- Given this information, which choice is the best one for you?

## You Always Have a Choice (continued)

- Why do you want to choose that?

- Now that you can see that it's a choice you are making, what's different?

- Can you own that choice as yours? Why or why not?

- What benefits do you see in taking ownership of it?

# WHAT ABOUT MOM?

## Beliefs About Self-Care

Your beliefs about self-care will impact how much (or how little) you practice it. People who believe self-care is necessary for their sense of well-being have an easy time making it a priority. Let's find out what you are thinking about it.

- Self-care is: _____.

- People who make self-care a #1 priority are _____.

- I would do more in terms of self-care if _____.

- When I think about making my own self-care my #1 priority, it feels _____.

- It would be easier to consider self-care a priority if _____.

## Beliefs About Self-Care (continued)

• When I do take good care of myself, I feel _____.

• The best thing about taking care of myself is _____.

## #1 Priority—Visualization

Visualizing how your life will improve is a great motivation for making changes. Let's take some time to see how your life might be different so you can decide if it's worth it.

- Think about the one area or concept you want to improve when it comes to self-care and write it here:

- Imagine making that your #1 priority. How would you feel if you made sure it happened for you?

- What would be different in your life?

- Who else might benefit from you making this change?

## #1 Priority—Visualization (continued)

• What would be easier?

• The best part about making this my #1 priority is _____.

## Self-Care Questionnaire

- On a scale from 1 to 10, how would you rate your overall self-care?

- Are you satisfied with this number? Why or why not?

- Name one self-care concept that you want to focus on:

- Why is this important to you?

- How would it make a difference in your life if you were able to implement this concept?

## Self-Care Questionnaire (continued)

- What ideas do you have to make this a priority?

- Are you willing to commit to putting this into practice? What exactly are you committing to? Please be very detailed.

## Physical Self-Care Inventory

- On a scale from 1 to 10, how would you rate your physical self-care?

- Are you satisfied with this number? Why or why not?

- Rate your satisfaction level on each of the following from 1 to 10.

  - Nutrition/hydration:

  - Rest:

  - Movement:

## Physical Self-Care Inventory (continued)

- Name one self-care concept or activity that you want to focus on:

- Why is this important to you?

- How will this make a difference in your life?

- What ideas do you have to make this a priority?

- Are you willing to commit to putting this into practice? What exactly are you committing to? Please be very detailed.

## Mental Self-Care Inventory

- On a scale from 1 to 10, how would you rate your mental self-care?

- Are you satisfied with this number? Why or why not?

- Rate your satisfaction level on each of the following from 1-10.

  o Continued learning:

  o Creativity:

  o Useful thought patterns:

  o Quiet/Mental rest:

## Mental Self-Care Inventory (continued)

- Name one self-care concept or activity that you want to focus on:

- Why is this important to you?

- How will this make a difference in your life?

- What ideas do you have to make this a priority?

- Are you willing to commit to putting this into practice? What exactly are you committing to? Please be very detailed.

## Emotional Self-Care Inventory

- On a scale from 1 to 10, how would you rate your emotional self-care?

- Are you satisfied with this number? Why or why not?

- Rate your satisfaction level on each of the following from 1 to 10.

  o Social connections:

  o Positive relationships:

  o Personal joy/Life satisfaction:

## Emotional Self-Care Inventory (continued)

- Name one self-care concept or activity that you want to focus on:

- Why is this important to you?

- How will this make a difference in your life?

- What ideas do you have to make this a priority?

- Are you willing to commit to putting this into practice? What exactly are you committing to? Please be very detailed.

## Spiritual Self-Care Inventory

- On a scale from 1 to 10, how would you rate your spiritual self-care?

- Are you satisfied with this number? Why or why not?

- Rate your satisfaction level on each of the following from 1 to 10.

  o Connection to your higher power:

  o Kind and loving self-talk:

  o Tuning into your needs:

## Spiritual Self-Care Inventory (continued)

• Name one self-care concept or activity that you want to focus on:

• Why is this important to you?

• How will this make a difference in your life?

• What ideas do you have to make this a priority?

• Are you willing to commit to putting this into practice? What exactly are you committing to? Please be very detailed.

## How Is Your Self-Talk?

The way you talk to yourself cultivates the type of relationship you have with yourself. That relationship lays the foundation for all other relationships in your life. Let's see how your self-talk looks.

- When you make a mistake on any given day, how do you talk to yourself about it?

- Are you happy with this? Why or why not?

- What are the best things you tell yourself on a daily basis?

- What are the worst things you say to yourself on a daily basis?

- Choose three things you'd like to tell yourself every day and write them here:

## How Is Your Self-Talk? (continued)

- If that self-talk became a habit, what would be different for you?



- How would you feel and what might you do as a result?

## What Do You Believe About You?

We all have beliefs about ourselves as far as what we deserve, what we are capable of, and who we are. It's important to take a look at what you believe and see if you want to believe that more is possible for you. Let's take a look.

• I believe I'm worthy of _____.

• I believe other people are worthy of _____.

• The type of people who want to be around me are _____.

• I'm not as good as people who have _____.

• I have more money than people who _____, but less money than people who _____.

## What Do You Believe About You? (continued)

- If anything were possible for me, I would believe I could have _____.

- If anything were possible for me, I would believe I could be _____.

- When you think that these beliefs can be changed and that you can be anything that you want, what is that like for you?

## Joy Inventory

Personal joy is an important part of good health! Let's see how much joy you create for yourself.

What are your top five sources of joy?

1.

2.

3.

4.

5.

## Joy Inventory (continued)

- How do you feel about this list?

- Do you need to diversify your joy more?

- What would you like your top source of joy to be?

- In what ways can you create joy internally? Give two examples:

## Mental Rehearsal: Looking to the Future

It's a lot of fun to think about the changes you want to make and imagine already having made them. It will inspire you and help you find the solutions to get there. Go ahead and visualize what's possible.

- Think about the changes you want to make in your life, and visualize yourself having already made them. What is different about you?

- How do you handle problems differently?

- How do you feel differently?

- How do you act differently?

- How do you show up differently?

## Mental Rehearsal: Looking to the Future (continued)

- When you imagine yourself "practicing" for this part in your new life, what are you doing well, and what do you need to keep practicing?

- How will you know when it has clicked for you?

# ABOUT THE AUTHOR

Molly Claire is a Master Certified Life Coach who is passionate about helping her clients achieve their greatest potential. Molly speaks, teaches, and coaches women from around the world and believes that as individuals change, so does the world.

Her business is merely an extension of how she feels about raising her kids—helping each of them to become who they are meant to be and create a fulfilling life. She is honored to have the opportunity to support women who make such a difference every day.

Molly has always had a keen interest in brain development, specifically in early childhood. During her years as a stay-at-home mom, she created preschool groups and taught at a private preschool, always implementing strategies to encourage healthy brain development.

When Molly found life coaching, she was amazed at how the cognitive process helped her change her life. That's when she knew that she wanted to help other women understand their brain as well and understand (and change) their lives.

Molly is double certified as a Master Life and Weight Loss Coach. She also trains coaches for The Life Coach School and walks with them side by side as they complete the certification process.

Molly is the proud mom of a musician, an athlete, and a strong-willed bundle of "sugar and spice" (heavy on the spice). They are her pride and joy. They challenge her daily and are her greatest teachers.

Molly Claire offers private and group coaching by phone, online, and through live retreats. Visit Molly's website at www.mollyclaire.com for free resources and to learn about *The Happy Mom Mindset* program, coaching, and podcast.

Made in the USA
Las Vegas, NV
20 February 2021